A CHAIR FOR ELIJAH

Menke Katz

illustrations by Lisa Smith

The Smith ✶ **New York**

First Edition—All Rights Reserved
Library of Congress Catalog Number: 85-061563
ISBN: 0-912292-77-6 (paper edition)

Printed at Capital City Press, Montpelier, VT
Typography by ETC Graphics, NYC

contents

contents

contents

For my great friends: My wife Rivke,
my daughter Troim, my son Heershe-Dovid;
my brothers Elchik, Berke, Yeiske, Meishke
and my sister Bloomke who always inspired
me to love life more, to believe that ages
beyond me will not forget me.

Forever your Menke

AT OUR FOREST HOUSE

LISTENING TO THE WIND

(for my daughter Troim)

O hear
the wind swear:
no, no, we shall
never die. Only
things made by demigods
die. We are infinite as
a bud, a worm, a dream. We shall
see light on earth as long as there is
a star in some undiscovered planet.

A CHAIR FOR ELIJAH

(for Rivke)

Solitude is God.
Let us hide in seven
heavens, at our forest house.
Only God and the beggar
Elijah are welcome guests.

We leave a chair for
Elijah who comes to us
to rest, weary from
his wanders, leaving at dusk
on a chariot of fire.

At dusk we see God
on our windowpanes as an
alchemist who turns
the gold of the dying day
into dream: a cosmos for two.

MARCH

No, March
does not come
like a lion,
but like a host to
invite us all: man, beast
bird, every worm born anew,
to celebrate our days and nights,
the lucky while on earth, to welcome
the woodchuck to the sun out of its dark
sleep, to greet the redwinged blackbirds, the singing
bridegrooms who fly before their brides to be able
to yearn for love: O kal-lee-lee, come O come
brides to join the chorus to March—the gem aquamarine.
The wedding guests are orioles, robins, brown thrashers,
invited is Shulamith from the Song of Songs,
Gifts are the crocus, (the boy in love with a
nymph) the blue violet—the fair maid, the
sap of the maple trees, the march of
all flowers of March against Mars:
the god of War. Apples in
bud return us all to
Eden, to drink a
toast to the last
as to the
first Spring.

WHEN BUDS OPEN

Lucky
lovers die
in March when
buds open to defy
death, thrilled with adventures
of the first taste of life. (O
hear all winds wailing over the
fate of a wounded bud, healed by God.)

Brooks break
the locks of
ice when the cries of
love of wild geese are
heard over rivers, line
their nests with their own down on
the same earth of which Adam was made.

EARLY SPRING

Early Spring. Peepers in marshes, cattails, rushes
are in love with twilight as robins with dawn.
Crocuses shelter hungry bees, their sting
delights as first love. Hear the call of
the treefrogs. Hi! Hepaticas
on the hillside are here to
prove there is life after
death. The long winter
hibernates in
graves in fear
of Spring.

WISE ACRE

Rainbows learned from drops of rain to live a moment or two with
the sun, with immortality and die—all delight. O
their death is miraculous as their lives. Butterflies:
goatweed emperors fly over a wise acre
to find a shortcut to heaven, bypath the
creeping ages of the turtles, detour
the dull wisdoms of the hoarding fool
the wizard who can change a star
into a flea, transfigure
a nightingale into
a cricket, can squeeze
the endlessness
into a
crawl space.

16

DIVINE SPIDER

I saw an orbweaver
on a gloaming pane
a recluse among spiders,
spinning a plunderless network,
entangling only
the evening star Venus
in its empty cobweb
a divine spider, happy
to be destitute of prey.

FIREFLY

A firefly is as
luminous as the Zohar,
a scholar of the
Book of Splendor, scintillates
the beginning, God's first light.

GOLDENROD

Late summer. Goldenrod joins the desperadoes of the fields:
briars, spines, wild roses, the thorn gangs which scratched the blush out
of the dolled-up violets. Mermaids meet them in the
mirrors of brooks, dusk bogs, deserted ponds; carefree
vagrants, they roam through forbidden soils until
the frost bends their bare rods into hoary
rainbows, until they moan and rattle
in the wind like phantom fiddlers
on their way to the ghostland.
Goldenrod, flower of
the wretched, of the
fallen angels,
the flag of
the cursed.

AUTUMN WHIM

Leaves fall
when they tire
of still life, each
leaf, in autumn, is
travel-mad, envious
of the leaves which are free of
the chains of the trees, find in the
wind true freedom. O ask any leaf
if life is ever ended after death.

Leaves reach
Paradise
in winds which
lift them in swift tongued
streams, start life afresh like
wee dreamboats for elf children.
Some sail West to escort the last
rays into the night. Some turn East in
infinite search for the unreachable dawn.

Some leaves
glide into
the end of all
tomorrows, lull in
wind and water: unborn
ages, find Eden where man
will seek the unknown, forever,
through luring daymares, until all will
flee like released leaves, running from their trees.

FORGET ME NOT

I daydream a hundred years hence, beyond my last laugh, wrath, cry.
I am a Forget-Me-Not on my long forgotten grave,
Spring-stricken, in my private sky, out of the blue I
see you, my little woman, a little cloud tired
of the heights, yearning for the rainburst—Menke!
Menke! O hear me call you Rivele:
glide down to me so we may be close
to each other as a dream in
a dream. The sky craves to reach
the earth as the earth the
sky. We vanish in
our own dreamland,
left is the
far cry:

        Forget
           Me
             Not!

EPITAPH

I am the lover
who drowned in the Viliya
river, swimming to
my love with a Forget-Me-
Not flower yearning in my hand.

AT OUR FOREST HOUSE

The bed
of milkweed
and thistledown
where the chipmunk slept
the winter away looks
yearnfully abandoned as
the bed which you left as if you
vanished in a distant century.
Left of you is the word love: a thorny
pillow to stab my dreams, to nail my lost stars.
The chipmunk still heavy with sleep stands on a stump
announcing like Messiah the end of death. Bees in
search of Spring taste the first golden grains of pollen: first love.

Evening. Last rays seek darkness to escape from their own light.
Longhorned grasshoppers shrill prayers to the end of day.
Only the deaf hear violets cry for help in
the teeth of weeds. Milkweeds nurse undernourished
stars of our bygone nights. An owl in a
pine tree bewails bird, beast, man, God, in
four, six, eight cries: whoo — hoo — hoo — hoo.
A red fox barks at vultures,
terrifies the heavens.
Autumn. Carrion
crows triumph through
the naked
forest.

WHIRLWIND

SNOWFALL IN BOROUGH PARK

Snowfall,
Borough Park
eats all its dumps
away. The crooked
roof of a poet's dream-
attic is like a hanging
garden of Babylon. Diseased
fruits, resting in the gutter, on their
way to hell, are in full blossom again.
A mouse—a homeless ghost, queen of the wretched
adorned with rare snowgems, wrought by God's personal
jewelsmith, runs to safety from its enemy light, to
its only friend—darkness; walled-in phantoms, petting their snow
beards, amuse it with the brightest gloom in newborn Borough Park.

TEMPEST IN BOROUGH PARK

Come my
love, it is
the same whirlwind
which took Elijah
to heaven. Some lightnings
convert into chariots,
some into fire-horses. Let us
meet God like Elijah, stormwashed, cleanse
the light where smiling horrormongers stood.
The tempest is weary, fearing sleep, it still
keeps alive by dancing horas on the tired streets,
with feet of dust, hands of wind, the sphinx of Borough Park.
Last drops of rain, through sunset, are rainbow chasers. Itchy
cats, with fleas in their ears, piss gold: the terror of the ages.

STORM

Quick tempered clouds move
by fits and starts bored of the
skies, break away like
sea monsters, armed with lightning,
thunderbolts, thrown by brute gods.

A storm—a nerve wrecked
leviathan, devours towns,
forests, leaves only
in myths winged snakes, clawed dragons.
The storm applauds its own might.

WINTER TRANCE

Dead streams are alive
with the stagnant might of mute
quagmires, with the gall
of swamp-apples, dream they are
babblers, cascades, waterfalls,

where naiads live. The
sunset transforms all the mud-
blisters into one
succulent trance, turns each swamp
into a cupful of wine.

WINTER RIVERS

Gay ice carnivals,
the festivals of carefree
rivers, celebrate
their seclusion under hoar
frost, rush to the freedom of

solitude, until
the hermit thrush, the angel
of the swamps is here
to sing of you and me, worm,
sky, bear and eagle alike.

SNOWFALL IN THE VILLAGE OF MICHALISHEK

Children in my dream
ful village saw in a snow
fall the celestial
hierarchy fall, every
snowflake—a fallen angel.

Some flakes were seraphs,
some—cherubs, some archangels.
Snow brought the crooked
alleys into heaven. Each
snowflake left a tear for the

poor synagogue mouse
and a kiss of peace
for the dust of the
nearby cemetery, the
Eden of my forefathers.

NEVERLAND

In the
wind on my
street, I hear the
voice of the organ
grinder, (all that is left
of him) Yankele Klesmer,
the alley musician of my
razed village. I hear the lone, sobbing
organ barrel ask God, beast, man, Satan:
which wing, which flying windmill, which distance can
reach you, my vanished village? Oi Michalishek,
my first love, my last tear, never dying neverland.

FOG

Even fogs are weary,
rest at the adjacent
stream, at our old forest
house, build fogbanks, circle
at twilight the yellow
arcs of fogbows, show still
unexplored, unknown stars.

Fog dogs bark at the moon
as it rises to chew
them from crest to their loins,
from knees to their elbows,
from their heads to their tails,
until left of every
dog is only the bark.

A flock of sage fogsheep,
their eyes blinded by their
own wool, escape without
a trace (in fear of man,
prince of slaughterhouses)
beyond God's creation,
to mother nothingness.

Fogs descend on earth to
share the fate of all plagued
mortals, drizzle with the
shed and unshed tears of
stones, man, turtles, destined
to pine since Adam, to
the end of the last dawn.

The wind sings hymns to
the deathful glory of
autumn. The dead summer
thrown on the rocks, listens:
O not an echo of
an echo will ever
be lost, my comely love.

LISTENING TO LITTLE RICHARD

(for Shelley and Claudia)

Little Richard, ye-ye-ye, true music is wonder and terror.
I hear winds rock and roll since the beginning of night and day.
True-true-true, music is storm-armed, splitting rocks—stoned ennui.
Music is earthquake, rising from under the sea to
topple cities. Music is a wave-gang shouting:
Little Richard roll and rock heaven and earth.
The cries of fallen angels in your voice.
Whipped prisoners shriek, in vain, for help.
Black slaves rush out of your blues, bind
their jailers in their own chains.
Africa marches, clap
warning hands, stamping
bare feet, drum to
triumph, to
first dawn.

O hear Little Richard shout between the devil and the deep blue sea:
ho-ho-ho, hoo-hoo-hoo, ha-ha-ha, music is a rage which sweeps
us all away, shock-waves rocking America, cities fall
over one another, Satan leading the dance of death,
Heaven-heaven-heaven, throwing Eden down-down-down.
Hell-hell-hell rolling in its own fire-storms, returns
the hundred and ninety six thousand worlds back
to pre-genesis darkness. New York is
the valley of hinnom; god moloch,
music-mad, applauds the cries of
dying children who rock and
roll on blazing altars.
Little Richard is
lulled in a bed
of lava.
Sha! Peace!

KIN OF SATAN

FRANCOIS VILLON

Poet,
saint, bandit,
Francois Villon,
you learned in the dark
dungeons of Paris, no
friend is as loyal as true
solitude, you saw death as the
"child of an angel." You saw a law-
loving, smiling ghoul at the kind gallows.
(O there are enough tears to nourish the tree
of the doomed. O the hangman hangs God on each noose.)

You saw
Flora the
bride of Spring, walk
out of your "Ballad
of the dead Ladies," to
elope with you in heaven.
You are the envy of every
hermit, praying to his star to be
buried like Moses in an unknown grave.
No tombstone betrays your whereabouts. O all
stones are your humble monuments, Francois Villon.

Who if
not the wind
is the roaming
vagabond-piper
to find your grave among
the cursed, to serenade your
life and death, in star-crazed nights when
somnambulists see your grave as a
brook rushing to the river of naiads:
maidens lucky to escape heaven and earth.

Angels
in love with
sin, cast out of
heaven, see your grave
as a tiny island
of Havilah where the gold
of the loneliest dusk is good,
(authentic gold of autumn leaves in
limbo) the solitude of suicides
who are condemned to lie at the gates of tears.

Satan
will ever
read your poems
to the residents
of hell, and I—a dead,
long forgotten poet will
rise from dust to listen, applaud
you with the zeal of each thundercloud,
but your foe, Mademoiselle de Bruyeres
left only her "romance with the devil's fart."

WATERGATE

O fellow mortals, let us guard our immortal guardians.
The cherry blossoms, in their midst, blush with the venom of
diamond rattlesnakes, their violets bite with the wrath
of mad dogteeth. O they may burglarize even
the ghost of Washington, bleed white the heavens
of Jefferson, Paine, Lincoln, may yet take
America on a last ride, may
cash the sun as the head of a
squealer, at the twilights of
Watergate where shadows
are masked angels, pledge
allegiance to
the saint of
Bluebeard.

BLUEBEARD'S CONFESSION

(twin tanka)

I am in love with
six murdered brides which I may
turn into gold calves,
harpoon-lilies, almighty
elephants, fashionable

nightmares. Beheaded
brides are shielded with peace belts;
they are therefore safe,
in the blues of my bluebeard,
in the arms of their lover.

ON SEEING A PRESIDENT AMONG
THE HORDES OF MY CITY

O to
be a stray
hermit, seeking
solitude among
the hordes of my city,
peace at the roar of steel, flesh,
iron as if carrion crows shrill
themselves hoarse, rout the light of day,
hurling hoorahs around their flockmaster,
the small time giant, the phony world beater,
the crowned ghoul of the dead soldiers of small time wars.

Come O come, my love, let us jump the guns which
guard the vendor of our lives. The dream is
our haven. Let us sail the wonder-
seas—the mirrors of the mirage
of the deserts. Let us meet
the end with every grace
of the beginning,
naked as first light,
as rosebuds,
as truth.

THE TRANSFORMATIONS OF
KING CHARLES THE FIRST

The
ghost of
beheaded
King Charles the First
lived a life of ease,
in the luxuriant
mirror of his fallen crown.
He held on to his last star as
a beggar to his last silver coin,
until it rolled away like a shrunken
head to his head-hunter Oliver Cromwell.
Even for a ghost of a ghost there is no end and
end, hence King Charles the First reincarnated into
a frolic little pig munching the goody goodies from
meadow snackbars. The god of piggies named it Oinky, oinking:
oink-oink-oink, no death is as handsome as a live little pig.

Night.
Oinky,
the little
pig, moonlit, dolled
with the honey of
windfall fortunes: a true
cherub, lured out of heaven
all cherubs, playing in hollow
trees, on shepherd reeds, on scented rain-
drops, serenading all beheaded kings,
all queens and piggies. When Oinky was slaughtered,
swallowed, digested, the gods sent it to the Land
of Nod. Still left of Oinky is its oink-oink to oink:
in the ears of the slaughterer long after the knife will
retire in peace, rust, guilt. O let us all say Amen, Selah!

SONNET TO A HATEMONGER

O you
are dauntless
as a robot
with an electric
soul, no wonder you hate
the stars which do all their chores
by candlelight. The vixen hides
in her den, the doe in her thicket,
dream their death away in fear of the wolf
and hunger moons, until they rise and shine: Spring
is here, but you, mighty as the evil eye of
an iron poetaster, with frogs in your throat, croak
your blues as you reap the wings off Keats' nightingale. Even
Jesus of Kansas must cower among your slimy lilies.

SUPER DUNG

You, I
and Amos
the herdsman were
made of common dust,
only the Germans were
made of super dung. O rise,
dead of all the graves since Adam,
unite! They may build gas chambers in
heaven, may make lampshades of the wings of
seraphim, the ancestors of the Jews, may
nail the son of Saint Mary to the cross again.

PRAYER TO SATAN

(of the Jews of Auschwitz)

Satan, angel of
the doomed, make us blind, let us
be eyeless, tearproof
bless us with darkness, shield us
from the cursed light of our days.

HANGMAN LAUGHING

I hear
a hangman
laughing. Mother,
where shall I hide from
his laughter? If I were
hidden in a den of a
wild forest, I would see the trees
in the wind like giggling gallows, would
see on each branch a noose for you and me.
His laughter mocks the cries of all the slaughtered.
In the fires of every sundown I am burnt at
stake. The moon over a death cell frightens the heavens
like the head of a hanged man. The last look of the
doomed haunts the newborn as well as the dying.
Carrion crows are lured to his laughter.
I hear earth-trembles, foreshock warnings
of earthquakes. I hear hurricanes,
typhoons, tornadoes roaring
for help. The night covers
us all with hooded
masks when we hear
a hangman
laughing.

ON ADAM

Adam was not chased
out of Eden, he escaped
like a convict out
of the sight of God to be
free as Satan in hell.

Adam
will return
to Eden when
the blessed wrecker will
raze the grief of the last
jail on earth. O see the sun:
a clock which tells of a dawn when
the last doomed will outdevil death and
let the cheated hangman hug the gallows.

COOKIE

Cookie,
dew on a
blade of grass, on
your grave, (in calm nights,
at moonfall) reminds of
gemmed earrings, fit for you O
frightened nightwalker, blushing whore,
novice in the oldest trade, on
the streets of Manhattan. I learned from you,
child-harlot, to see the invisible tears
of a ragged doll, thrown in the gutter, praying
to the god of dolls with a mouth—a mudheap. O dolls,
trodden children in a dream with the dust of heaven on
their clothes, dolls—jewelweeds, adorned God's throne before the fall of man.

SUNDOWN ON THE OLD STREET

Skyborn
alchemists
turn the twilight
slums into goldarn
castles. Genesis: as
if God created heaven
and earth at dusk, here on the old
street. Adam is a booze hound, drinking
lechaim to hell. Eve is a lucky
whore, angels spit pennies from heaven; Eden
is a bait cherry under her tattered figleaf.
A pimp—a serpent, dressed to kill, entwines the old street.
My punky room is a giant's mirror where I, ages
hence, live in wonder tales of the village of Michalishek.

OLD STREET

The day—airsick, blind,
is begging crumbs of light from
the star-paved, old street.

PIMPS IN HEAVEN

Pimps sneak out of hell
to lure angels into their
underground brothels.

FALSE MESSIAH

Whores wake the dead, shout:
resurrection! Two bits for
a heavenly screw.

LILITH

Lilith will be the
last whore on earth, the last life
of the last race. She
will rape God, will give birth to
heavenless, bastard angels.

BYGONE SUMMER

Autumn. Katydids
in shrubs bemoan the sad nights.
A dead bird holds in
its wings the bygone summer.
Bushes rattle in the wind

your shattered promise
of infinite love. A deer
runs to God for help
at the sight of the hunter.
God falls, lies shot like the deer.

AFTER THE HUNT

Empty nests are wounds
in the woods. It seems even
the sun was downed by
the hunter, even stones bleed.
The wind, at rest, stooped in grief.

Evil calm. I hear
the unsung songs of a mute
song-thrush, God under
its stiff wings. The last shriek will
echo its doom to ends of time.

Hunter, the closed beak
may yet open to peck your
skull in dream terrors
when a hag with nine ghouls will
crown you as their ghastly chief.

EARTHWORM

The blind earthworm has
ten hearts, no wonder, it is
so kind as if it
were born only to be bait
in the hands of fishermen.

O hear the prayer
of the earthworm: God of worms,
your earth is soiled sin,
your heaven—the haven for
the apostles of Satan.

Deprived of light, wings,
why did you bereave me of
the claws of the beast?
Help me cheat all cheats, to hook
the hookers on their own hooks.

O give the Garden
of Eden to all who are
sinless as the worm.
Even Moses was not as
guiltless as the pious worm.

ON LOVE

Learn love from the eyeful scorpion,
who sees love with its dozen eyes;
to be true, only when it
is twinned with the hate of
its poison-toothed
sting, against all
enemies
of life.

TO MY BROTHERS YEISKE AND MEISHKE

Brothers,
we are all
born for autumn,
harvest. Autumn leads
the symphony of seasons,
if the child April still plays
the frolics of fool's day, (O let
us blossom in autumn as in May.)
if June is still the bride of brides. Ours is
the nectar of the last flowers of summer:
the rayed asters, the autumn crocus. Whitefooted
mice are still here to garner the ripe summer. Ours is
the scent of bruised cherries, the owl's hoot, the rhythm of the
wistful ebbtides, our nearby snowbed is crystalline wonder.

BEREAVED MOTHER

Autumn.
The bereaved
mother against
the dying day of
Manhattan sees all the
bridges burn in the sunset,
beyond her, still left is a bridge
of sighs, built of fog, dust, blood, mistfall
where she sees her son—an unknown soldier,
a medaled ghost crossing the shadowland to
receive homage of his honorable archfiends,
for his valor of dying unknown as if he were
cradled by a sterile wind—the mother of nothingness.

She says:
my son, good
to know, not you
but I who died with
you will die again. She
sees God entangled in the
corroded steel of razed cities,
hears mountain and dale winds chat with her
bygone century. She sees all unknown
soldiers swarm out of their graves to join the fire-
eaten universe. She sees the end of all ends
the end of war, end of peace, O the end of all ends.

MODERN LULLABY

Die, my
little child,
die, O die, all
good, nameless children
obey their mothers and
die before they are born. Yours
is the kindest of all angels,
the angel of death. Sleep, O sleep, my
little child, graves and children do not blend.
My womb is your motherly grave to avoid
the mourn of dust. Only naughty, unborn children
whine down into the surgical trash, O bypass life,
O reach paradise, all virtue, all sinproof, as a child
in a dream, in the safe arms of God. You are all Spring, rushing
with the first streams after every ray of
your unrisen dawns, running after the fancy of your
quenched sunsets. All stars will keep forever the light of
your eyes. All birds will always keep featherbeds for
you under their wings. All stones will soothe your end
less night with mute lullabies which only
the unborn can hear: ai-le-loo-le
loo-le-loo. Your prayers are in
every breeze: God, I am all
light, seeking in vain the
live darkness, all good,
bereaved of the
grand sins of
the earth.

UNDER THE HUNTER'S MOON

Autumn.
The last fly
of the summer
asks a speck of dust
what life is like beyond
death. The fly dies, turns into
a dream, outruns the speed of light.
My clock harnessed to go backwards on
its way to reach Adam, ticktocks moments
more infinite than time. Midnight. Out of the
hunter's moon come to me all the children who were
doomed before they were born, attack me like falling stars.
Children—mocked people who live in a dream of a dream.
I hear their unheard cries like the squeaks of trapped mice
which throw God off his throne. O unborn children,
if you came to me to demand life, then
take my body made of swan song. Hence
they tear me limb by limb, until
left of me is only null,
fear times fear, only this
poem which unborn
children wrote for
the hunter's
full moon.

MOONLIT WINDOWPANE

The cries of unborn children who live in the seventh heaven
outcry the midnight prayers in the awestricken almshouse.
Through the moonlit windowpane Messiah is riding
on a cloud: two seraphim at his right, two—left.
At the second wail of the ram's horn all the
dead rise. Even slaughtered lambs bleat again,
to teach kindness to the knives which killed
them. Messiah is infinite
dawn. Death died. All winds in a
jubilant race bring the
angel of death to
his own last grave
beyond night
and day.

LOVERS OF EVIL

O the army of Satan's soldiers, lovers of evil: archfiends,
began a war against God, attacked the Garden of Eden,
seized the flaming sword which turned every way to guard the tree
of life, cut the three pairs of wings of the seraphim,
left all angels wingless, encircled the throne of
God. Fogdogs devoured demons in a tooth to
tooth combat, in contending nightmares of
Yahweh. Chimeras joined to vomit
flames, setting fires to the seven
heavens, seven earths, left of
Eden a ruin-heap.
God in everloved
solitude hid
from Satan's
cursed mob.

Still left was the tree of good and evil, in the wrecked Eden where
God sat in fierce meditation, saw a world without graves where
only death will die, without sin or virtue, without hell
on earth or in heaven, a world of poets, builders,
dreamers. Out of nowhere came the serpent on two
feet, the height of a camel, Eve's first true pal,
hissed in fear: "Help! Satan is still here!"

Envoy

O hear old storms battle storms. See
crawling angels mock God, jeer
Isaiah, the prince of
peace, left is the sword
to rule heaven,
earth. Left is
Satan.

THE WITCH OF BOROUGH PARK

(tanka)

The witch of Borough
Park mixed in her witches' brew
my last, handsomest
sunsets, drove my late dreamboat
through fire, the pirate of dreams.

The fire burst into
bloom, each blaze—a rose of Pig
Street. Ye, a true witch
flew over me on a broom,
night and day until she swept

me into a charmed
bottle. I am a corked soul
damned to call for help
until the last cry on earth,
until Messiah will come.

Each star—an evil
eye sees me in revels of
the witches' sabbat
in gloom of midnight when they
swear allegiance to the lord

of flies: Beelzebub,
as they tear me asunder,
limb by limb, until
left of me are only nails
torn out of my toes, fingers.

Stars are in constant
search for loopholes to escape
the skies like the eyes
of the doomed seeking freedom
through the bars of their deathcells.

The witch of Borough
Park applauds with cheering
hands as she sees me
vanish like cursed smoke through the
chimneys of the gas chambers

where the lovers of
the dreams of my potato
village burned alive.
O save me gracious Satan
from the witch of Borough Park!

42

PRAYER OF A FLY

(six line Tanka)

June night. Galaxies
of angels heard the unheard
whining of a fly:
doomed in a star-struck cobweb:
We brought you seven heavens,
the wonders of Genesis.

The fly forlorn in
the universe of angels,
at the jaws of the
spider, zoomed its last prayer:
vanish angels, curse me not
with love—my arch enemy.

Bless me with the claws
of evil to fight the net-
monger, to tear the
silk gallows spun with fine
fingers of death, to scratch all
the eyes out of the spider.

Not the sterile love
of angels, not the embrace
of spiders, give me
the bite of the black widow,
the fangs of the copperhead.
O divine sin of Satan!

A FLY IN HEAVEN

A fly confesses
all its sins to the spider:
I stole a lick of
honey. I disturbed the calm
with my zoom, announcing Spring.

The spider, silkrobed
scanned each crime with its eight eyes
and said: I shall save
your soul from this sin-loved earth,
my cobweb is your heaven.

MIDNIGHT SERENADE

(ballade in six line tanka)

Calm in the village
is armed with storm. Amy of
proud beggar stock,
since the birth of the village,
is in love with the star-eyed
cemetery—home of man.

She sees her lover
Todres, the organ grinder,
chief concert master
of Beggar Alley leave his
grave to tell her that their love
is endless—endless like God.

She hears the wind—the
street musician grinding the
organ to amuse
the dead: O the end of time
reached her timeless village. O
come O come, rush Messiah:

The Torah is sealed
with mildew. Wolves run from the
burning forest of
Zaborchi. Not Jews, frogs in
red swamps pray to the new moon:
the sickle in reaper's hands.

Todres, I am the
last one to cry to the deaf
heavens. The empty
alleys are populated
with ghosts. Adam dies dusk in,
dusk out on a firebed.

A daisy (day's eye)
in her hands withers away.
The petals slip out
of her fingers—scentful death.
She is the living fear on
the love-struck cemetery.

O Todres, I hear
you serenade me from your
grave. O let me share
a nook with you in heaven.
O let me be a pillow
under your head, my lover.

The castle-like church
is leveled to the ground.
The moon—a white shroud
over the wrecked synagogue.
God, homeless, wanders lonely
through the ruins of the village.

PSALM AT MIDNIGHT

The shouting streets of
cities echo the cries of
my burning village.

Left of you and me,
heaven, earth, Eden and hell
is only the night.

The night no dawn may
ever touch, the night in the
eyeholes of the blind,

the night under the
horror masks of the doomed, the
night Prince Satan rules.

O ashes of my
chosen people! O we are
eternal like the night

which may never see
a star, the night before the
birth and end of God.

O the night without
life or death like the unknown
dreams of the unborn.

IN THE YEAR OF
THREE THOUSAND AND ONE
(on the atomic war)

The vision of Menke, the son of Heershe Dovid,
the poet of potato folk of the village
of Michalishek. I see the end of all
life on earth, in the year of three thousand
and one: end of man, bird, king, hangmen.
The unborn welcome all beyond
time. Winds will telltale of a
bygone world. Not an ear
left to listen. God
will hide in fear
of the thug:
Satan.

THE ROCK

THE ROCK

Moses,
the rock which
you hurt in the
wilderness will not
forgive you, will call you
to justice on the day when
Messiah will come to proclaim
the end of death (O then only death
will die) O see the rock every sundown
as your own wound which even God cannot heal.

Moses,
God's wrath was
in the waters
which flowed out of the
rock to quench the thirsty
centuries of the desert.
Only the rock heard God say: O
Moses, you my equal who spoke to
me forty days and forty nights, face to
face, my chum, dared to strike a dumb stricken rock!

Moses,
prince of the
prophets, you did
not learn from Jacob
the shepherd to see a
rock like a pillow for the
weary wanderer who built in
dreams ladders for moon-led angels to
ascend and descend from birth unto death,—
hence, you reached the land of Nod, not of promise.

At the
end of days,
the bruised rock will
show its scars to God,
will demand that you be
driven out of Eden for
slapping a rock blessed with the peace
of inanimate heavens, until
guiltsick you will hear the rock howling in
the winds, with the speechless anguish of the mute.

AN OPEN LETTER TO KING SOLOMON

Who if not a whoremonger would see vanity of
vanities, after tiring of seven hundred
nude princesses who danced down the hills to you
like mooncrowned oreads, everyone with
a navel like a round goblet which
needed no wine and three hundred
concubines who bathed for you,
in enchanted brooks like
naiads, everyone
with an arse, ripe
as a heap
of wheat.

Where are the keys to your forty nine gates of wisdom?
O fool, slave of Moloch—the god who threw children
into fire lured your thousand maidens, each one
a rose of Sharon vied to be the first
bride of your orgy nights. Hear the wise
crickets eulogize your glory
with all their praise: cri-cric-ket.
Crickets will chirp to the
last autumn on earth:
So-lo-mon, slave
of gods. King
of fools.

ON SIMON BAR YOHAI

Each rock reminds of the cave where Simon Bar Yohai
wrote the Zohar—the Book of Splendor. O bless me
God to turn into a rock, in the midst of
our rivulet, rushing to the glory
of end-all, it will tell me of the
light hidden in the wise darkness.
Our busy stream will not tire
to confide the unknown.
The rock—a hump of
patience will not
weary to listen.

FALL OF A TREE
(for my brother Berke)

The tree
that fell in
a storm attack,
left for me the pain
of each torn root, the wounds
of the sapwood, thirst of the
leafbuds, the cry of the fallen
crown. All trees of the forest lament
the lost world like blind mourners without tears.

RETURN TO THE VILLAGE OF MICHALISHEK

1.

When Velfke the mystic returned from every hell on earth, in
shreds and patches to a heap of burnt ruins which was once
the singing village of Michalishek, he saw like
Abraham, when thrown into fire, each flame—a rose
of resurrection. He saw his ancestors:
proud-blooded beggars slink out of the scorched
ages, their tears mixed with the ashes
of Beggar Alley. The aching
silence outhowled hungry wolves
in the moonlit fright of
the forest. Feathers
of a devoured
crow haunted
the wind.

2.

Velfke the mystic saw God: a guest in heaven as man on earth.
He saw God dying with the last ray of deathful sunset.
God was a dead beggar begging life from the dust to which
all his creations returned. O if Yankele the
needle-nosed tailor were alive he would sew a
divine shroud for God but now he must lie shroud-
less with all the dead in the downed summer,
in the naked autumn. Gabriel
flew out of Daniel's visions,
embracing with his kind wings
God's Edenful being,
cried Kaddish with the
first and last life
on earth: God
is dead.

3.

Velfke the mystic stood like a fablemonger
listening to a tempest—a thousand roared curse
against God, terrorizing the storm-lit
heavens, shouting out time and space: Down
wretched angels, winged traitors of
dreams. He heard each thunderbolt
proclaim he is God's heir
to rule the hollow
heavens, the world
of each flea
on earth.

4.

Velfke the mystic saw Messiah over God's invisible
grave eulogize the dead king of life and death: God you drowned in
your sins. When I, the son of David will come, you will rise
like all the dead, to atone to every worm, man, beast.
Only then you may say the light of the first dawn
is good, only heaven without hell is good,
only the earth without grief is good. He
saw Messiah leaving, bound to his
oath to return at the end of
night and day. A lost crowd of
fallen angels like stray
waifs chummed with dancing
little bears—the
playfolk of
the woods.

MARCH OF THE DEAD

(for my father Heershe Dovid and my mother Badane)

I call upon all the Jews in heaven and on earth to join the march
of the dead—a death-march against God for playing deaf at the
wailing of our comely folks, gassed in the gas chambers of
Auschwitz, Treblinka, Ponar as he sat throned in the
rare luxuries of Eden. O see my dauntless
ancestors in the God awful march, waving
prayer shawls like flag alarms. Sad little
shoes of dead children knock-knock, march-march.
The living and the dead stride in
measured steps through the valley
of Hinnom, until God
leaves the heavens, joins
the endless
death march.

PRAYER TO SIN

1.
I died
a hundred
years ago, at
our forest house, in
Spring Glen. My last day did
not end like a flickering
candle in the wind. I saw my
last sundown splendorous as my first
dawn. The angel of death was a welcome
guest. I followed him beyond tears and laughter.
Now, after five score in heaven I die again
of divine boredom. Menke, the champion lover on
earth, after a hundred years is like a sterile angel.
O hear my prayer, curse me God, to be heavenless as sin.

2.
Only
kind Satan,
my friend, since my
first cry against cries,
clenched my prayer in aid,
led me to a bride-bed on
a shabby street of slummed New York
to marry a while my love who was
nursed by motherless breasts, cradled by the
fate of Job, promise-bound for good luck pennies
to love me in a trice forever, against a
tower-torn sky. O in hell, I shall name her Eden.

MOTHER TONGUE

(for my son Dovid)

Wherever Yiddish
is mute as the dust on my
grave, spoken only

by dust-mouths in the
wind, there I never lived or
died, was never born.

Wherever Yiddish
mingles with the ashes of
my scorched village there

crawl wingless angels,
there will weep God to the end
of his creation.

O hear my mother-
tongue in Spring, in the busy
brook, see it winter

adorn with frost dreams
the windowpanes of the birch
hut where I was born.

O meet my uncle
Chaim the blacksmith when he
hears the iron speak

Yiddish on firebeds
as Moses heard God's voice out
of the Burning Bush.

VOICES OF CALM

When you come to my grave listen to the calm.
You will hear me thinking of you, yearning
for a chat, simple talk, as dust to
dust, wind to wind. See me all light,
forever sunrise. Only
the never-never born
are darkness beyond
Genesis on
the face of
the deep.

Learn from daylilies to live longer from dawn
to sundown than the turtle or the life
of dull Methuselah: nine hundred and
sixty nine years. Raise a cup of
wine over my grave and say:
Lechaim to Menke.
Lilith, my love, will
join you and say:
Lechaim
to hell!

O every frog will croak lechaim to me.
Harvest flies will zoom lechaim to my
bygone summers. Every stone will hear
my headstone say lechaim to me.
Death is the fib of the dust-
devil. If I am a
blade of grass I am
industrious
as a great
city.

Fallen Autumn leaves, await
Messiah as you and
I, the return to the
dream of dreams, to
mother of Eve,
first dawn.

A RAINBOW OR TWO

MY SISTER BLOOMKE

My love-
lorn, widowed
sister Bloomke,
learned to weep from the
weeping willows: silent
mourners born at the longing
bank of the Viliya river
which hugged the village, its bosom friend,
night and day around its hoarse cuckoo clocks.
The weeping willows prospered until they reached
the patched windowholes of the house where she was born.
She learned hospitality from the willows as they
gave their generous shade to weary beggars who wandered
ages through the bare distances of Lithuania, gaunt
paupers, rich with the crumbs of kindly bread in their beggar bags,
always ready to share their wealth with birds, mice, fish in the
lucky waters of the village where her forefathers
nourished centuries of love, hate, fought wolves in the
wild forests, kicked the noble guts out of the
robber barons, laughed, cried, died, leaving their
widows look at the black tails of the
widow-birds like veils, famishing
the light of withered summers.
She saw the first budbreak
commune with the end,
with the fallen
star, with the
blindworm.

TO A POETASTER

Poe
taster
eunuch of
the muse in the
harem of the nine
concubines of song who
scintillate in jewelled cliches.
O circus duck, puny rhymester!

PRAISE TO THE
RHYMES OF JOHN KEATS

Praise to the "mused rhyme"
of John Keats, crown of poets.
Rhymes of sound heartbeat
flow through the ages, star-led,
like the river of heaven.

John Keats, I am like
you, "in love with easeful death"
when I hear the song
of your nightingale, reaching
the first and last dawn on earth.

Your nightingale hops
from line to line as from dream
to dream, a pause at
every rhyme to listen to
your night-scented ode—to song.

O your nightingale
lured lovely Ruth out of the
Bible from a moon-
glade field which seemed like ever
chased waves in a midnight sea,

oared by cherubs, rhymed
in harmony of the spheres.
Your song charmed all the
angels out of heaven as
though of hemlock they had drunk.

AGAINST LOCK OR RHYME

Poems,
sit in rhymes
like men, birds, beasts
in cages. I saw
Samson with fist in the
teeth of a lion, forced to
his knees under the load of rhymes.

Poet,
brother, let
your word roll un-
rhymed as thunder, let
it flash like free lightning
through the fog: over a parched
field, the eager harbinger of
rain. The poem in rhyme bends like a
captured enemy under an arched yoke.

A chased deer in panic of the forest does
not race in rhyme, a grieved stone does not mourn in rhyme.
The rhyme, patted, rounded by the file of crystal verse,
cuts into the flesh of a word like a wound. If like thirst,
stream, sun, storm is eternal the poem, lock not the storm in
the cell of a rhyme. Give the word the fresh scent of ripe corn,
swaying in wind of a hopeful field, tasty as rare
bread of my hungry childhood. Let the word ride on,
speak face to face with your neighbor of a far
century. Wars do not kill in rhyme. A
plummeting airplane like a wounded
eagle does not fall in rhyme. A
hurricane does not uproot
trees in rhyme. A stormy
sea is a rhymeless
call for a day
without lock
or rhyme.

PORTRAIT OF A GRAPHOMANIAC

All words hate his guts:
words like manna falling from
heaven in deserts;
words—lost winds in distress, cry
for help as they rush to God.

A cliche juggler,
tossing, catching the worn moon
until the sky is
haunted by the face of a
ghoul, feeding on its own corpse.

A slytongued barker,
outbarks chased foxes, outshrieks
laughs of hyenas,
prowls through his own heavens, preys
on cherubs as on winged rats.

White impatiens faint
in fear of his touch. Sundowns
suicide in their
own fires. Moses in nightmares
chews cud like a beardless goat.

Lilacs weep as they
drink his dew made in wordmills.
Narcissus bows in
awe, all mirrors are in love
with his fabled reflection.

A dazzling selfist,
his grandeur leaves shame-eaten
the modest daylight,
or the scented nights of June,
bereaved of his own shadow.

He is faultless as
a wooden frog, crowned king of
kings of beams. His star
gurgles in shampoos, moral
pimp of harlot damselflies.

Pal of Baudelaire's
old whores who outblush flame-cheeked
paper roses; masked
like Pope, "he perfumes the skies"
from the top of Mount Carmel.

A horned sorcerer,
he transforms golden eagles
into fleahoppers;
sends evil spirits to milk
the breasts of virgin Mary.

He hocus-pocussed
his own universe where clouds
burst into inkstorms,
smirch with ink his soul as if
he were born in an inkhole.

TO A TRUTHMONGER

The cruelest of all
beasts is your naked truth. You
transform me into
a mule, a wolf-spider, a
yak, zebu, a snake-idol.

O you are all truth,
bladed as a slaughtering
knife over my throat,
and there is no ram in sight
to offer his life for me.

I am the prince of
liars. On my travels through
back ages, I reached
beyond God, dueled Adam,
fled from Eden with nude Eve.

At dawn, Eve was half
woman, half fish, made of a
fake rib when she heard:
Trick or treat, the picklock of
the truth of all truths is here.

O savage-hearted
truth, you see me as a kind
monster whose gift is
a tin apple for a starved
tear-kissed bride in famine land.

Is truth a blind god
with eyes like potato warts;
who digs lies like gems;
would love my head, guillotined,
set on a headless dragon?

My last lie will be
in mirror-writing on my
gravestone at a stray
sun: rising, falling nowhere,
reaching everywhere.

TO RIVKE

Rocks with
faces of
gods bathe in our
stream, at the side road.
Ours is the secure shade
of the old forest house. The
roving waters will serenade
you centuries beyond our last dusk.

Twilight.
O even
serpents are now
peaceful as rainbows.
Rivulets play love with
each other, coalesce in
constant embrace. Naiads reared in
our stream, lulled in rockbeds, lullaby

our son's
yet unborn
children. Waters
rush on in diverse
cycles, the echoes pine
away craving each other.
Even the stinkweeds are not love-
proof, are in love with their own shadows.

Let us
run amuck
from the throngs of
great white ways, mobs of
cities are like desert
locusts. Solitude is here
the guardian angel of our
love, my mellow eyed little woman.

WINDBEATEN LAURELS

(for Rivke)

Come, my love on my
grave in your wedding dress with
a goblet of wine.

Hear me speak to you
from my tombstone: a stone out
tongues all languages.

O hear beyond me
my unwritten poems: hymns
to you in the wind.

O hear, my love, all
winds serenade us until
the end, end and end

ON SOLITUDE

The lie and the roar
live in hordes. God and the mouse,
I and the love-sick
and jackals howling against
the stars yearn in solitude.

CITY CLOUD

I saw a cloud turn
into an old wolf who broke
the last tooth, biting
the claws of a steel dragon
of New York—queen of cities.

WAITING AT TWILIGHT

I see you die on
each towerpane, buried in
underground rushlands.

Night. My earful room
listens to the silence of
your vanished steps.

POET LAUREATE

A spider is here to weave a crown for me, its poet laureate.
My deserted poems play solitaire in the moonlit garret.
Seraphim fly on six wings of fire through haunted crevices,
guard the throne of God. A moonborn maiden reads my poems
to listening walls, then hides them beyond my last dawn,
like unknown treasures in the deepest sea of dreams.
Frostwork plants a dream forest on each window
pane, builds a wondrous hut from the tree of
Eden for me and you—my maiden,
to spin an endless yarn of love,
till the wind—a weeping flute
will eulogize the end
of you and me, end
of heaven, earth,
and of Song
of Songs.

DARK STAR

(for my cousin who committed suicide)

Night. O listen, the
wind is the cry of the mute,
the whipped mouth of the
doomed, praying to a dark star:
Come death, kindest of angels.

ON THE ROADSIDE
(for Ethel)

I came here on the roadside, across your grave to return
your visits to me. The grass is well fed on your grave.
Leafbuds flower in daymares. Daylilies are loved
by the dying sun, by their only bygone
day—the span of all life on earth. Damselflies shrill one note songs as they patrol
the quick tempered brook. A mouse runs
to demand of God equal
rights on earth, calls on all
mice to face the sun,
to march against
the foe of
God—man.

Solitary wasps: masons, carpenters, diggers—miners,
mud daubers—potters mix their saliva with mud to
form mortar to build urns. All neighbors are welcome
to torment, paralyze spiders, dissect life,
rear with the delicacies their young. Fire
beetles star the nightfall. Memories
crowd to conquer death, to reach my
love. Gooseberries smell of jam,
pies, tart and you. The wood
thrush sings to remind
the psalmists, they
learned to psalm
from birds.

Autumn.
Leaves in a
danse macabre,
celebrate their own
death, until at rest, guard
the dreams of the roots, the sap
of the earth. Rains bewail entombed
summers. The angel Raphael flies
over the graves to heal the dead. Winter.
The four winds are packs of wolves. The coldest moon
of the year: a clowned face of mock eternity,
laughs at you and me, at life and death, Eden and hell.

LONG WINTER NIGHT

Winter,
night, snow, sky,
yearning. I am
the lover, spurned by
the loveless goddess of
love as if she were forged by
the god-smith of my village, the
almighty maker of tin-souled gods.

I stand
at your house
like a snowman.
Your door, forever
locked, the key thrown away.
The night is undying as
if the archfiend of hangmen downed
the sun into a noose with nine turns.

It seems
Satan said:
"There shall be no
light. The day shall not
rise again." (Stars are un-
touchable dimes to tease
homeless beggars.) A dog howls to
the heavens God's ineffable name.

O small
wonder then,
my strength is of
the golem shaped by
the cabalist of Prague.
Samson is in my long hair.
I can throw down all the pillars
of tower and town with my bare hands.

PARAGOOLT

Frostwork
adorns each
windowpane with
a girl out of
the snow-white tales, waiting
for me, the poet of Pig
Street, in a dream of a dream. Winds
do not tire calling her: Paragoolt.

Who are
you, my love
Paragoolt, far
and near girl? From which
past or future age
did you come? —Do not ask my
lover, you see, I was born on
a windowpane. Frost is my mother.

At dawn
I saw you
melting, my love,
on all windowpanes,
in a thousand and one
suns. O such light may be seen
by a dying goddess before
she falls from Eden to Eden.

Left of
me is a
snowbeard on a
street of old New York.
Left of you, my lost dream:
Paragoolt is a stone-eyed
tear which mirrors two lovers who
swear infinite love in their twin grave.

FALLEN ANGEL

The fallen angel
Shemhazai, damned by God to
hang between heaven
and earth forever, his head
downward as a sleeping bat,

for his sin to love
the fairest maiden on earth
Ishtehar. O he
yearns for her, age in, age out.
O who hears his call for her

through weeping whirlwinds?
Who knows his daymares, at
the end of ends he
craves to turn into dawn? Who
hears his prayers night and day

for a glance at her,
a touch, a kiss: dream to dream?
Who O who if not
Satan, the kindest of all
angels is at his downfall?

Under the wings of
Satan, the fallen angel
Shemhazai with his
love Istehar eloped to
Spring Glen—the earthbound Eden.

APRIL ALLEY

(for my brother Elchik)

Late twilight. Barefoot children enchant Pig Street,
fly through straws, rainbows of soap. Two lovers:
Elchik and Dveirke charm the skyworn
village walking through the dreams of
the beggars' dreamland. Dveirke:
thin-wristed, crocus-fresh,
April-scented, her
love ribbons green
her braids in
three strands.

The rowan tree awaiting red-lit berries,
saves from mischief of evil-eye women.
The small white flowers are childish cool.
The full eyed moon bathes in the depths
of the Viliya river.
Dveirke loosened her long
hair to reach the grace
of her ankles.
April; birth
of buds.

Reb Moishe, the night owl seeks darkness to give
light to the blind riddles of the Zohar.
Dveirke hears the wind lull tomorrow's
children. Night. She is safe even
from death in her lover's arms.
The distance echoes with
the voices of the
unborn, with old
harps of new
Jubals.

MY LAST PRAYER

Thank you God that I
see my last sunset, that I
will be grass, stone, night.

O lead me beyond
the first or last life on earth,
beyond the unborn.
O thank you God that I will
still be in every rainbow.

EULOGY

My love,
the winds will
never stop their
endless wander, will
never cease searching, in
vain, a trace of everyone
of us, after the last bye-bye
of man, beast, worm, eagle, you and me
and the mouse. Meet me in the beautiful
darkness beyond the first beginning, before
there was night and day, sin, tears and graves, life and death,
before all the just evil of the punishing God.
Only the unborn are the blest in heaven and on earth,
safe from Eden and hell. Let us find the world of the unborn.

ON RESURRECTION

We shall
all be born
again, among
the unborn: a dream
without the dreamer. Like
God each one will be neither
end nor beginning, neither night
nor day. Timeless as the world before
Genesis, before time. Spaceless, we shall
be everywhere and nowhere: nonexistent
existence in worm and angel, in dust and sky.

THE THIRTEENTH LABOR

Hercules' thirteenth labor was to turn into a fly, snarled in
the noose of a cobweb and wing out as the king of giants,
but the fly fought, in vain, to free itself of the death trap.
A star sneaked into the cobweb to swear eternal
love to the fly. A host of stars followed, changed the
cobweb into a heaven of light. The fly
prayed to every star: O vanish my love,
death is a spider with Satan's eyes,
silk fingers. Let my enemy
hide me in night shrouds. Your light
outhorrors all deaths. — — — Then,
mighty Hercules:
a dead fly, met
his true love—
darkness.

NOBLE DUST

Dust refused to turn
into man, the image of
the sword of Duma
the angel of Gehenna,
hence God made Adam of light.

SEVEN

Wonder
times wonder
is seven. There
are seven heavens,
seven earths, seven seas,
seven worlds. Seven women
get hold of one man's balls in the
far nonevil land of Isaiah.
Seven sleepers of Ephesus sleep two
hundred years in a cave of the Koran.
Seven, seven et cetera, et cetera.

ON DARKNESS

Darkness in the wise
Zohar has the zeal of
the first and the last
light on earth. Learn from darkness
the lambent language of fire.

Darkness like God has
the face of the abyss, the
unfathomable
light which blind Homer saw in
Iliad and Odyssey.

BEYOND NINETEEN EIGHTY NINE

I died in the year
of nineteen eighty nine. All
life on earth and
in heaven died in me. Without
life, even God is Godless.

I am alive as
hope, as dust of which Adam
was made, young as
the youngest darkness before
there was light, sorrow, mirth: world.

There is not a ghost
here in this sky-born ghostland.
Time—the only ghoul
who robbed all my nights and days
is now timeless as I am.

Good to be free of
good and evil, free even
of death for none of
us here beyond our last step
are aware that we are dead.

I shall wait for the
second call of Messiah
when all the dead will
rise and all the graves will bloom,
in the Garden of Eden.

I shall be Menke
again, chat, light winged, with friends,
at a wine table,
drink lechaim in heaven
to my love of long ago.

THOUGHTS OF A SLEEPWALKER

Who if not a star
may light the thoughts of gravestones,
the dreams of the dead.

Let us hide my love
from our own ghosts: in Eden,
on earth or in hell.

FROM THE TREE OF KNOWLEDGE

My son, learn to love
solitude like God before
he created time,
the fate of man: Job and boils
and the island universe.

Learn philosophy
from a wounded wolf, howling
to God and the stars.
Learn to meditate from old
gravestones, moss-crowned, muse-ridden.

TWILIGHT REVERIES

Twilight. The busy
brook, across the road, rocks my
last day to sleep. I
see you, Dovid, my son, my
beginning beyond the end.

All ships are bored with
the seas, every ship which drowns,
commits suicide.
All trees doomed to stand
ages, pray to death since birth.

I see a shot bird
fall into a fairytale.
I see all rivers
hurry, to be swallowed by
the arid thirsty deserts.

I hear in the wind
a thousand times a thousand
criers announce the
end of all life on earth: man,
skunk, nightingale: kin of dust.

Satan is here to
wake sleeping tornadoes, to
rise against heaven,
down the throne of the old God.
Time to elect a new God.

The new God without
you and me, without good and
evil, without life,
death, will die of solitude.
Calm will outhowl bygone storms.

THOUGHTS AT NIGHTFALL

I am in love with
darkness, the mystic maiden
who lives in Zohar.
I learned from the blind to see
all wonderworlds through darkness.

I learned from the mute
the language which God taught stones,
the voice of silence.
The mute: laugh, cry, pray and ache
like the stone which Moses hit.

Some minutes are dawns.
Some moments are falling stars.
A joymonger is
hidden in every sorrow,
sorrow lurks through every joy.

When Messiah will
come, beasts—the higher angels
will lead all hunters
out of the forests, to show
them the way to nearby God.

WAITING FOR ETHEL

New York is rushing
under the earth, climbs over
and over Babel.

A flowerpot in my
bachelor room faded to the
last summer's endbud.

Come O come Ethel:
My room is nerveridden with
your silence. O come!

Moments are eager
ears which pine away for the
echoes of your steps.

Which storm can outhowl
this silence? O I am a
roomful of yearning.

A speck of dust is
a crumb of eternity.
Who am I, life, death?

Darkness wavers, falls.
God says: there shall be light and
hi-ho, you appear!

GRAVES

Graves are live specks of
the universe, whirl around
the sun, rush through space,
to reach you, me, to meet on
a white donkey Messiah.

ON OLD AGE

Learn to
revere the
glorious dusk
of old age. The chill
of the last days of the
summer is blessed with harvest.
The farthest distances are the
closest. Dreams are real as root and sap.
April Fool is seen on September hill
tops. The senses are keen as of the woodchuck
who smells November a moon ahead. The end is
sacred as the dust of which Adam is made. Be prompt
for reaping as a ripe apple of Eden. Solitude
will outlive heaven, darkness is infinite as the unknown.

MY UNCLE BENTKE, PRINCE OF CARDS

Crown of my family-tree on the magic carpet of cards.
Your servants were kings, queens who reigned under you: fate-gambler.
The sun rose and fell in your royal flush of poker.
Cards laugh, cry, love, hate. Cards—gifts of the gods, dreamers
found treasures hidden in rich dreams. Cards—dreamboats
sailed through never-seas where aces ruled life
and death. Goddesses of fate obeyed
your command to load with fire, brim
stone, even your dud cards, to
destine for poker-faced
hicks, cards like death-bells,—
ring downfall. O
wizard of
wizards!

Bentke, eighty year old prankster what can you do in heaven,
if not tickle pink the angels until they are laughing jack
asses, play pinochle with seraphim as they guard
God's throne, win all the stars until the heavens are
blind and you play solitaire in limbo when
kicked out of hell. Come O come Bentke, I
hear the winds shuffle your nights and days
like packs of cards, each card dreams of
your spellbound fingertips as
a sleeping beauty of
the touch of her prince
charming in an
enchanted
castle.

ON GRASS

We die,
so we may
be humble as
grass. Flowers fade to
be free of ornaments,
like grass. True queens without crowns
may not flirt with their own idle
vanities. O we all die to pollinate like the wind
the starry grasslands of the eternal fields.

ON MY POEMS

My poems are eternal as the night in the dark garret
of our forest house. One season is destined for June as
well as December, one fate for the beginning as
for the end. A time-weary star seeking death through
rain or snow-scarred cracks is welcome forever
by the generous darkness. O who if
not spiders will read here my poems?
(If God will teach them to read.) O
find me, my love, beyond my
last kiss with teeth, claws of
my poems in a
jarring clash with
dust-eaten
dreamworlds.

WEEPING WILLOWS

Weeping
willows bowed
with grief of the
starless. O hear the
cries of the mute when they
are slapped by autumn winds; struck
with sorrow even in April
when the long death of winter dies and
their sadness is budding warm as their sap,
as the anguished love of eternal mourners.

I saw
the moonmad
somnambulist
embraced by the drooped
branches of a weeping
willow as by the entranced
arms of Morpheus, god of dreams,
as he leads them over the towers
of Babel: New York, climbing sky eater,
the Jerusalem of the heavens on earth.

Weeping
willows keep
guard over the
enchanted brook where
Cinderella leaves her
fairytale to bathe at dusk,
to share her cindered beauty with
the wood nymphs who lull her to sleep in
her starred waterbed, dreaming of a world
shaped like the lost shoe which her prince charming found
in the lucky bag of her fairy godmother.

No, not
the wreath of
laurel, mine is
the sad glory of
the weeping willow, the
sorrowful garland which may
laureate the unknown poets,
the creators of their own skies, the
hermits who marry the weeping willows,
lovers of divine loneliness which only
a desert-mouse, a rock, a cave-bat understands.

SWAN SONG

Autumn.
The season
of death is all
mine. Mine is the dusk
which will tarry into
my last dawn. I am dying
sun in, sun out in full splendor.

O there
is as much
wonder in the
last flame as in the
first. My brief visit on
earth is at the end of its
dragline, wrung of joy and sorrow.

I see
my days strewn
like home-driven
leaves, in the teeth of
the wind, under Satan's feet.
Eternal is the same-sized
sing-song of the robin in May.

Timeproof
are the mass
gabbling geese in
October. God walks
in solitude (lured by
my poem) on the lonely
track of the terror-struck field mouse.

O who
if not the
dying swan taught
ecclesiastes,
(the king of the preachers)
vanity of vanities:
the true Song of Songs, the swan song.

Brother
of ages
hence, O hear the
grim reaper calling
your name, persistent as
mine, as the drab choir of the
crickets, in long autumn nights.

SONG

No, it is not all
vanity my son. My end
is your beginning.

I shall never be
stone-asleep, a sterile mute.
Silence is all song.

Hear next year's crickets
still in their eggs, serenade
all future autumns.

TO MY SON HEERSHE DOVID

IN THE YEAR OF TWO THOUSAND

Dovid,
my twenty
eight year old son,
good to see you in
the year of two thousand,
in mid-August of your life,
when I will be a near and far
memory to you. O I know how
I will yearn for you, biting my own dust.

You may
still dream of
me as a torn
leaf dreams in wind to
return to its father
tree. You may see my poems
burn, in late autumn, in the sad,
flickering gold of the tamaracks,
before the needles fall in splendid death.

O see
my life cleansed
by the brisk light
of the first frost, at
dusk, when the scorched sun wheels
as a windfall apple, hear
me calling you as a brook locked
beneath ice: O-Ho Heershe Dovid
you are beyond my last night, my first dawn.

CHANT MENKE

Heershe-
Dovid, son
of my every
longing, each wonder,
handsome as my poems.
I write these lines to you in
dull Borough Park, at midnight. Stray
cats meow the birds and Spring away.
The moonborn angels guard the ailanthus,
the tree of Brooklyn-gods—the tree of heaven.

Angels
in squalor
of our backyard,
fly the tree through the
dreams of haunted forests
which scare the ax out of the
woodchopper's hands, break asunder
the unbreakable wings of death. The
polluted cherubim walk arm in arm
with unborn brides playing love under the eaves.

O see my poems made of your and my bone,
of your and my marrow, touch the nerveroots
of my restless similes, like the
fires of torches through night and wind
and you will know that you are
I, and I am—you, a
selfsame twin, half of
you, born two score
and ten years
before.

We are
both children,
astray in an
enchanted forest
where the deer and hunter
are pals, butcher knives break bread
with God, kill birthday cakes, slaughter
apples, fruit of Eden, though I hear
wild geese cry that hunters will plow the fields
with guns, until winds will tire of their wander.

I see
kings, hangmen,
presidents, bores,
bumpkins, descendants
of the first serpent on
earth, their evil cleansed by the
sly tongues of lickspits, the hawk-eyed
peddlers of tears, booming the thriving
prosperity of graves, wreathe Old Glory
into bouquets of ghosts, of all dead soldiers.

Envoy

I pledge
allegiance
to the flag of
true hermits, escape
the fanfare of mobs, drums
the many-headed hooray
screechers, see the sun as a gold
medal which is the multiface of
death. Let us avoid Lucifer's bleak laws,
all hermits pray to the god of the unknown.

ON MEETING MY SON'S GRANDCHILD

I will
meet death—the
truth of all truths
four years hence, my son.
I will see all my days
dwindle in the distance—a
dark speck will leave the dream endless.
A far away hand will wave to me
farewell. It will not be the end of
me. Some falling star will give me its last light.

My son, I met beyond my last thought of you
one of your unborn grandchildren who will
be the Poet Laureate of my
life and death, a dream's throw from here,
a dream, authentic as the
days which will dawn beyond
me. I said: your name
like mine shall be
Menke, my
choice name,

exquisite as belladonna, the deadly
nightshade with poisonous berries which doomed
the comely folks on the starved fields of
my childhood, the name with the guts
of a rose, hewed out of rock:
Rockrose, born in fires of
my Burning Village,
still dreaming of
the Land of
Manna.

TO MY SON'S GRANDCHILD MENKE

(from Menke to Menke)

Hello
Menke, my
Great Grand poet,
I will shake your hand
at the next century
when I am dust-fed, when skies
will wallow in the blues of all
my bygone Junes. Hi, Menke, I see
you unravel Genesis again though
every dawn is only a rainbow or two

from the
end of all
life on earth. All
storms howl for rest, all
beginnings seek their end.
Every Babel falls stone-eared
as I did, as you, the stars, the
maggots, goat-gods will. O we are all
wretched kings whose only crowns are tombstones.
O weave of my sunsets the dawn of all dawns.

I see
the seeds of
belladonnas,
glory of my sins
ride to you through the wind,
to bring you my every mood-
print. You are my first blush, my last
laugh, yearning, wrath, my handsome evil.

Learn joy
from lucky
fish who never
saw cursed nets, frolic
in water-ballets, seek
the mystery of depths they
own since Genesis, dumbfounded
with the wonder of God's creation.

See me
rich with all
the gold mines of
Autumn, hear me in
choirs of crickets surpass
all opera pomp, welcome
me among the crows who will
come to winter on naked hilltops.

Envoy

See no
miracle
miraculous
as the eyeful light
of a deer, just after
it outraced the fire of the
hunter's bullets. I may be the
deer who cheated death, call him Menke.

O FIND ME, MENKE, AMONG ALL GOD'S CHILDREN

O find
me Menke
among all God's
children, born like you
and I, toothless, naked,
blind: the velvet-eyed mouse, the
squirrel—the champion acrobat,
sent to amuse us and the angels.

Listen
not to the
nightingale which
caused Keats' heart to ache,
hear me in piping calls
of tree-toads—marsh angels (where
stars bathe in swamps—baths of heaven)
to tell you: Spring is here! I am here!

I may
be the chum
of a star-skunk,
at the brook of our
old forest house, with fur
marbled of dawn and night, then
see me as a rare bud. Even
a stinkard may break into flower.

I may
transmigrate
as a baby-
pig, then see, Menke,
all piggies as dolls which
only God can create, then
see no castle as princely as
the hutch where the mother pig gives birth.

It may
be I will
reincarnate
into Isaiah's
wolf, blessed with peace, grazing
on the fields of tomorrow
my own summers, and you—the child
to lead even Satan to Eden.

Envoy

I leave in my poems: mice and dreams, stars and thorns
and forget-me-nots for you my son, Heershe-
Dovid and your Grand Poet Menke.
You will both follow the blazing trails
of my vanished dreams, until you
will both sneak out of Eden,
I out of hell, for a sad,
coffeeless chat which
stones and mutes will
understand.
Good night.

Final Envoy

Stranger,
should you by
chance, stray to my
deserted grave, stop!
Listen! My headstone bent
under the yoke of ages,
communes with every silence on earth.
O legend, my never, never home.

THOUGHTS IN A FURNISHED ROOM

DARWIN IN A FURNISHED ROOM AT MIDNIGHT

(a study of cockroaches)

I see Darwin walk out of his godless
heaven on a moonlit windowpane,
bowing to every cockroach of
this bleak room, he says: Hi! grandfolk
roaches, forefathers of
man, survival of
the fittest. Hail
makers of
Adam.

All stars join the army of cockroaches,
as they march out of their dark, moist cracks.
American cockroaches, great
Yankees, star-struck travelers
of unknown seas, among
the first sailors with
Columbus to
find a world
in dreams.

Cockroaches trained in speed by mother night,
since the first buds burst in bloom on their
family tree, two hundred and
eighty million years ago.
Bedbugs panic, fear of
being devoured, grubs
are welcome to
the gloom of
midnight.

O sport fans of America, let us
cheer the champion roaches which outrace
here all wingless creatures, such as
blister mites, seeking to gall
pear trees, under the bed;
jumping spiders which
court their brides with
dance around
their prey.

June bugs, aristocratic fig eaters
begin a race-riot, surround the
frightened lamp, menace the rights of
stinkbugs. Dawn. As if touched by
King Midas, all bugs wear
gold tails. Even the
sun rises here as
a goldarn
cockroach.

Cockroaches are the true citizens of
the world, dine at the homemade dung of
India as well as at the
starlit garbage of New York;
roaches loved by the moon
since dust fought God, spurned
his command to
turn into
mankind.

A FURNISHED ROOM AT SUNSET

It seems
God weary
of heaven and
earth chose to die here
on the windowpanes of
the garret, in this cheerless
rooming house. I see God fall as
if stabbed by a thug who robs all the
gold of all the dying days, since Adam.

Angels
scale the room,
to weave a wreath
of forget-me-nots,
which fade ages on the
wallpaper gnawed by sterile
termites. Socrates on a blurred
painting still holds his cup of hemlock
drinking a toast to the condemned sun.

A lost
pigeon strays
between blind walls
(which climb against the
curse of Babel) cooing:
God is dead! The wings dyed with
smoke, it flutters through hell of brick,
din, steel, back to the Eden of its
first ancestor, to the wild-wood rock dove.

GOD ON ETERNITY

The skies are weary
as I am of heavenly
drudgery. I yearn
to elude eternity.
O if I could create a

judge or a monster
to destine me to die like
you, the worm, (Even
the worm is my own image.)
or the blue forget me not.

GOD ON TRUTH

True is
the soothing
sleep of the un
biased dust before
I created Adam.
True is the loneliness of
the unknown hermit, true is the
nonexistence of the unborn. True
is my pet angel—death who may free me
of the chains of infinity. True is Prince
Satan who may help me return even Eden
to waste and void, to darkness. True is the solitude
with the face of the deep, my only companion star. O
condemned worm, let us change fates, you be—God, I the lucky worm.

SEGANZAGAEL

I heard the prince of wisdom: Seganzagael
say: Darkness is Elohim, hence there was light
only before there was God, before there
was Sheol, before there were graves on
earth. We shall all live in Eden
when God will vanish beyond
his own birth. Hear the prince
of wisdom say: God
failed, let us crown
Satan, the
god of hell.

ON MESSIAH

Messiah is in no hurry to come for he fears to give
even to himself infinity. He would rather be
the donkey on which he is destined to ride at the
end of days and let the donkey be Messiah
braying as through a ram's horn, calling all the
dead to dawn, all equals: man, bird, frog, God.
The doomed will be the first to rise, to
live their days which were once whipped, caged, choked.
The garden of Eden will
be on the once cursed earth,
where there were jails, hang
men, presidents,
gallows, wars,
heroes.

ON THE SINS OF GOD

God of mercy, are you not merciless to turn into dust
your own image to place as guards the Cherubim and the
flaming sword, to keep Eden locked, to create hell in
heaven after hell on earth for the only sin
of tasting one of your all-wise apples (fit
for a miser, hoarder of apples)? King
of the universe, would it not be
just to lead yourself through all the
torments of Gehenna to
atone for your wrongs since
Adam, until man
of true mercy
will forgive
your sins?

PRAYER OF THE ANGELS

God, we
are weary
of paradise,
of flying through dull
heavens since Genesis,
without ever tasting the
madness of scorched thirst of love or
hate, on the fascinating evils
of the earth. Save us from eternity,
the champion of immortal boredom. We fly
through time with the same tedium as the turtles
crawling through the stupor of sheltered nothingness. Give
us tears to bemoan our fate, for our eyes are tearless as
mute, caressed dolls which envy the cries of spanked pranksters. Give us
buttocks which hurt under a motherly rod. We are over
fed with virtue, we are now lovers of sin. O lead us
through the gehennas of the earth, so we may learn the
skill of throwing off the scent of the hound with teeth
trained in legal prey, in chase of the condemned,
the fugitives from Satan, runaways
from the chains of broken commandments,
handsome with your image. Bless us
out of pitiless divines.
Let us join the angels,
cast out of heaven,
share each bruise of
children born
in hell.

END OF DAY

QUEENS OF AUTUMN

Yeah, old
women are
the true queens of
autumn as they see
their twilights turn into
starlight. Crickets serenade
their wistful evenings. Old women
are comeliest when dressed in the full
glory of the autumn colors. Their walk
is beautiful among goldenrods with stems
like wands, carried by elves, dolled for the jubilees
of their diamond weddings. Even May is a cousin
of autumn. The buzz of hungry bees reminds of a lost
lover. They hear his voice in the song of the oriole, his
nectar still on their tongues is enough to fill with honey the
cup and saucer vine. They see faded blossoms bud into
seed again. Their memories scent of meadow-saffron.
Their fingers are queenly in white, green or purple
sapphires. Days gather like birds in restless flocks
ready to migrate. It is good to die
in May when cushions of grass and beds
of dandelion grow best, their blind
dates with fate, at sunset, is
all crystalline; rooted
in legends like gnarled
trees, bearing fruit
of a new
blest age.

BEYOND ALL BEYONDS

I will learn from stones the language of silence.
On a bare field, I will be an empty
pod dreaming of lost blossoms of gone-
by summers. A last autumn fly
straying through its night of doom
will touch me like darkness,
to share the end-all,
as if it were
the last life
on earth.

Mine will be heaven and earth. Winter brooks
under ice will rush me to the first
beginning, beyond all beyonds.
I will hear seeds fight for life
in the womb of the earth.
In an injured haw
thorn, I will smart
like a wound,
like hope.

The last hour like the first is all wonder
like the opening of infant buds of
marsh marigolds. Each dusk embraces
dawn: an eternal love in life
as well as in death, through rise
and fall of ages. O
my love, let us not
lose a trace of
the marvels
of death.

HAIKU

A drunk at twilight,
a ragged Midas sees in
his dreams dung turn into gold.

NIGHT VISION

Midnight.
Is it a
sleepwalker, a
god of dreams, climbing
through the mugged June night to
reach the crown of the tallest
tower of my splendrous city?

No, it
is a self
murderer, a
friend of death, falling
like a wingless eagle;
his own death, his only prey,
the gutter, his only heaven.

MARION

Among all the guests
around your hospital bed,
I saw death, lovely

as you Marion,
brimming with delight: Heaven!
Fly me to heaven!

Little tree frogs love
sunsets, robins—dawn. You are
in love with heaven.

If heaven is all
darkness, no wonder is as
wondrous as darkness.

If heaven is dust,
we are miraculous as
a span of God's dust.

If heaven is the
end, no beginning is as
lucky as the end.

If heaven is home
for all, from Adam to the
end of man, beast, stars,

let us all go home,
to mother-heaven, joyrapt
like you, Marion.

Twilight. The late sun
rolls away like a lost wheel,
beyond the beyond.

Heaven! Heaven is
a hand in the wind, waving
a last, last good-bye.

HUNGER

(for Clara)

God,
I am
so hungry
for death but it
is not in sight as
if there were a famine
of death. O fill my cup and
let me say lechaim to death.

WINTER NIGHT OF
OUR LORD HOOVER
(for Yehudis)

Night, terror, end-all.
The mother hangs on her homemade obliging noose. On the
cold jawed rope will new light of
an old Hoover day soon dawn.

Her child awakes in
a world—a marvelmonger,
without fear, without
crying havoc: a frostman drives
toy trains on the windowpanes.

The cradle is a
dreamboat sailing through a mooned
ocean of milk. The
mother sways as on a see
saw, up and down, down and up.

The child yells: hi! hi!
The mother is all wonder.
Her arms are a
cherub's wings. The noose is of
an elf enchanted braid.

The mother in near
by Eden sees her child lead
God's hordes through stormrent
skies to a new earth, to hang
the sun on a new axis.

BEYOND MY LAST WINTER

I will be a first
Spring. As a newborn child is
new with life, I will
be new with death, free of good,
evil, fortune, misfortune.

Sunset. The late day
on fire commits suicide.
Not to life, to death
let us sing Hallelujah.
O hear the wind say: Amen.

If I turn into
a living maggot, I
am mightier than a
dead Hercules, kinglier
than Zeus, fibbed king of gods.

Thank you God that I
am dust again, grass again,
I am you again:
the light of snowstorms, the voice
of rainbursts: the first rainbow.

UNNAMED

In the blindest night
lurks an eye of dawn. A last
shadow and a first
ray are twins. O see a last
tear in every first laughter.

ON CRUELTY AND KINDNESS

O what is as cruel
as the light of the rising
sun over my grave?

What is as kind as
the dust which will blind God, sole
creator of graves?

GRAND TOAST

As I reach King David's age, it is good to die
next to the first and the last love of all true
poets: solitude, in a lonely room
where I may not hear the last song of
a dying swan but the squeaking
serenade of a trapped mouse,
in a backyard of old
New York or in a
dream-gutter like
the gloried
drunk Poe.

Or may I die here in our old forest house,
when the redwinged blackbirds start to migrate.
My last thoughts littered with unwritten
poems, lulled into hell (No,
not the dull splendor
of Eden) by the
legends flowing
through the near
by creek.

Curse me not God to die in a hospital bed.
No darkness frightens like the light of snow white
hospital sheets like neat and trim shrouds, fit
for dying men who lie as on a
mercy display, under the wings
of the angel of death, led
to heaven by snobbish
hands of rubbersouled
doctors, as dusk
bleeds beyond
Adam.

And guard me God against the merciful eyes of
nurses who may see my penis, not as the
god of love who can thrill with fire from
the first to the last Eve on earth but
as a torn tail which can not raise
itself to frighten even
a horsefly away, un
like Socrates, may
I drink alone
a grand toast
to death.

DUSKMARES

This is my last dusk
on earth. Tomorrow I will
not even know I
am dust that I ever lived
or died or was ever born.

The sun falls from its
orbit. Last duskmares struggle
for their lives, in vain.
Only a wound is left of
all yesterdays, yesternights.

O hear the wind tell
of my good and my evil:
my hellbent wonders.
I am zero-zero, the
true twin of never-never.

A knifed moon is the
half face of a ghoul. My love
in a dream—mother
of Eve returns the world to
the beginning, beyond God.

END OF DAY

Twilight. A bumble
bee in late October hides
from death in a bur
marigold, praying to the
god of bumblebees for one

more last flight to end
the day with a moment of
beginning. Even
God is tired of living at
the end of day, end of ends.